STORY
LOVE
WORKBOOK

Trading in Religion for Discipleship

by F. Barton Davis

WWW.JESUSLOVESTORY.COM

F. Barton Davis

Love Story Workbook

Trading in Religion for Discipleship

www.jesuslovestory.com

Scriptures taken from the Holy Bible, New International Version®, NIV®. Copyright © 1973, 1978, 1984, 2011 by Biblica, Inc.™ Used by permission of Zondervan. All rights reserved worldwide. The "NIV" and "New International Version" are trademarks registered in the United States Patent and Trademark Office by Biblica, Inc.™

Love Story

Copyright © 2017 by F. Barton Davis

Published by Magi Media Publications

1675 Southpointe Dr.

Hoover Al 35244

All rights reserved. No part of this book may be duplicated, copied, translated, reproduced, or stored mechanically or electronically without the specific, written permission of Magi Media Publications.

Printed in the United States

Cover design: Brian Moore, Bmoe LLC

Interior design: Magi Media Publications

ISBN 978-0-9819502-6-6

To my lovely wife Michelle, my best friend and personal hero. You make me better and call me higher, through good times and bad. I thank God for blessing me with you and our special love and for our two amazing daughters, Jacquelyn and Kenya, who make our Love Story complete.

WWW.JESUSLOVESTORY.COM

Contents

Foreward 1
Chapter 1 **The End of Religion** 3
Chapter 2 **Formal Introductions** 6
Chapter 3 **The Love Letter** 14
Chapter 4 **Crazy In Love** 19
Chapter 5 **Being Exclusive** 23
Chapter 6 **The Engagement** 27
Chapter 7 **The Wedding** 32
Chapter 8 **Meet the Family** 37
Chapter 9 **Next Steps** 41
Bibliography 43

WWW.JESUSLOVESTORY.COM

Foreword

I've been surrounded by disciple-makers for almost thirty years. By the grace of God, I have developed friendships with many church leaders, church planters and missionaries-men and women who exhibit true devotion to God through countless acts of faith, courage, and sacrifice.

For the last fourteen years, it's been an honor to call Frank a friend. He lives with a rarely seen passion to know Christ and make him known. His devotion to the Lord isn't simply displayed by the churches he's helped plant nor the possessions he's sold to live overseas as a missionary. His faith in God's love is revealed by his posture during suffering, trial, and hardship. No matter what life or Satan has thrown his way, he refuses to doubt the love and power of God. I've often pondered the origin of his stubborn belief in God, thinking, "What in the world did he hear, see, or experience that sparked this unquenchable fire for the Lord?" Well, *Love Story* answers that question and more.

Ready for a bold proclamation? Here it goes: I know the material in this book is life changing. How do I know? It's not because it changed my life - which it has. And it's not because I've watched these lessons transform the hopelessly fallible from diverse backgrounds into the faithful few - which I have. I'm able to say that with confidence because this book is not from Frank. It's from the Holy Spirit inspired word of God. This new book contains the world's oldest story, the story of God's love for you.

Love Story will help you reciprocate that love to God as well. Many people have heard the greatest command (to love the Lord with all your heart, soul, mind and strength, Mk 12:28-31). But what does that look like? How is it possible to love someone you can't see or touch physically with most of your heart, let alone all? *Love Story* can help you see the feasibility and reality of that command in your life.

This story is for everyone. If you're tired of stale religion, this book is for you. For those looking for a sure foundation to build a life of faithfulness upon, this book can guide you. If you're discouraged by modern day Christendom, flooded with watered down devotion, and seek to be a part of the solution, this can equip you. And for those who are stagnant in their faith, distracted by worries, and plagued by unholy living, these lessons can strengthen and restore you.

I've been guilty of reading through books like this with contempt, rushing to get through the material and skipping the questions it asks. I encourage you to give the *Love Story* your heart. Strive to read with fresh eyes - eyes filled with hope. If you do, you'll open the door for God to transform you from a believer to a disciple of Jesus who makes disciples.

Ronnie Rose

Evangelist

First Rock Church (Greenville, SC)

WWW.JESUSLOVESTORY.COM

Chapter 1

The End of Religion

I grew up a religious kid in a religious family. Everyone in my family (my mom, my siblings, my grandparents, my cousins…everyone) believed in God, believed in Jesus, and even though many of us rarely read it, we believed in the Bible. On Sunday mornings, we went to church, and while I enjoyed church most of the time, it wasn't as if I had a choice. My mom was amazing but she was old school. She didn't give timeouts for unruly children; she gave knockouts and she did not negotiate with prepubescent terrorists. Mom said, "Go," so we went and saying, "I'm not going," wasn't ever going be a pleasant experience. Church was an acquired taste, but we learned to like it.

The first thing I did when I went away to college was to stop attending church. I still believed in God but I just didn't see how attending was going to get me closer to Him. Besides, from my point of view, I had learned what I needed to learn. I had used my astonishing powers of discernment to pick out the best lessons from all the denominations I had visited and leave the useless stuff behind. In my mind, I was the most spiritual guy I knew. I wore a cross every day, was quick to defend Christianity in debates with my *less enlightened* friends, and I read the Bible a couple of times a year with every intention of reading it more often. I had been baptized, gone through several other Catholic sacraments, and, for good measure, had prayed Jesus into my heart when I was in junior high school and again a time or two in high school. I was a pretty moral dude, not one of those weird Jesus Freaks going door to door, but I was a good guy. I had dotted my religious i's and crossed my t's. I was fine. I was covered. There was just one problem. If I was honest, truly honest, I was miserable.

I was the good kid, the nice guy, the high achiever, but all of that was a *mask*, and by the end of my freshmen year of college, I was exhausted with the weight of wearing it. The real me was filled with anger and so much fear. I was a religious guy from a religious family and it meant absolutely nothing. Religion couldn't help me; it couldn't console me; it couldn't make me whole. Religion couldn't heal the hurt, bitterness, and rejection that was growing inside me, devouring the best parts of me, yearning to break free. Religion is a lie.

There is a reason why many of the most bitter, most judgmental, most miserable folks that you will ever meet are also among the most religious. Religion breaks hearts; it doesn't heal them. It causes wars; it doesn't end them. It leads people away from God, not toward Him. Religion is a lie. It is an empty promise that imprisons rather than empowers.

Now, I'm not suggesting that God is a lie or that faith in Him is futile. I believe that true religion, that fosters intimacy with the Almighty, has the power to totally transform lives. The brand of religion that I am referencing in this chapter is outside in spirituality, instead of inside out, constantly consumed with the appearance of holiness rather than internal transformation. It is the type that evolves when conviction is buried under tradition and routine. Rather than being the place we come to find God, church has become an endless maze that makes it difficult to see Him, let alone connect with Him. To complicate matters further, in too many instances, faith is inherited instead of inspired, and the truth is that faith that is inherited is not faith at all. I experienced this emptiness in my youth.

Jesus is the answer, but He is not found in that kind of shallow spirituality. Jesus did not come to start a new religion. There were many creeds, dogmas, cults, and sects in Judea when He walked the earth. The last thing He came to do was to start a new one, called Christianity. Jesus came for a totally different reason. Jesus came to put an end to religion.

Through the days of Jesus's life, He showed us something better, truer than religion, nailing the old way to the cross and empowering a new path through the empty tomb. He offers relationship, not ritual, a vibrant, dynamic relationship with God through Christ. Just as Enoch walked with God, God wants to walk with you and me, and the door, the guide, the light, and the bridge to make that relationship a reality is Jesus.

It was during my sophomore year at the University of Maryland that God got my attention. I was dragged to a small Bible study group and what I found changed my life. I found people filled with Christ's love that loved me and accepted me from day one. It was a life-giving group, part of a life-giving campus ministry, where Christianity wasn't just a religion; it was a true relationship with God. It was there that I first encountered the real Jesus and saw the power of personal discipleship and one another love. I was saved shortly after that, and over time, God moved my heart to go into the full-time ministry. Why? Because I was convinced that there were men and women just like me who were wandering around angry, lost, and empty. Like me, they needed more than a church. They needed Jesus. I met my incredible wife, Michelle, in New York a few years after graduation and together we've spent the last twenty-nine years as church planters and missionaries.

That small Bible study group saved my life and changed the entire course of it. What those brothers and sisters helped me to discover is exactly what the book, *Love Story*, and this *Love Story Workbook* strive to pass on to you. My goal is to assist you in using the scriptures to connect with God on a relational level. My prayer is that you will come to experience a Lord who loves you with unshakable passion and will learn not only how to love Him in return but how to let that love radiate throughout every aspect of your life.

The approach of *Love Story* is to use the analogy of the stages of a romantic relationship to transport readers on a journey of discovery that will ignite a personal rapport with the Creator. This workbook is designed to be a companion work that enhances the experience of reading *Love Story*. It can help you fall in love with God for the first time, or for those who have a walk with Him, *Love Story* is great way to strengthen and/or rekindle the bond that already exists. Read on, embrace the *Love Story*, and let Jesus transform your mind and soul as you embark on the adventure of true discipleship. It is time to trade in religion for something more.

Lesson One

Question #1: True religion, as outlined in the Bible, will bring us closer to God. Unfortunately, many of us have experienced forms of religion that fall short. What have your experiences been with organized religion? With Christianity?

_____
_____
_____
_____

Question #2: What was positive about your religious experience? What was negative?

_____
_____
_____
_____

Question #3: How much do you believe that tradition plays a role of shaping the faith of people?

_____
_____
_____
_____

Question #4: In your opinion, is the influence of tradition a good or bad thing? Why or why not?

_____

Chapter 2

Formal Introductions

Every great romance has a story and every story has a beginning. A first meeting, the first date, the first kiss, each courtship has a series of firsts that spark the bond that changes both lives, forever. Whether the person with whom someone eventually falls in love is an individual that he/she has known for a while or a blind date, the movement from acquaintance, to like, to love, is always a winding road that often involves an *Aha* moment. I remember mine.

I met my future wife, Michelle, in New York. (she's a native New Yorker). We attended the same church and lived in the Bronx in the same neighborhood; in fact, her building was about one hundred feet from mine. Sometimes, we even waited at the same bus stop and caught the same bus on the way to work (more about that next chapter). Not only did we have many of the same friends, I was pretty close to one of her best friends and had been on dates with several ladies in Michelle's circle. I knew her; she knew me, on a superficial level, but we really hadn't truly met nor had a conversation longer than ten minutes. Most of what I knew about Michelle was what I had heard from other people; most of whom were telling me that I should take her out. Being stubborn and slow to figure out what's good for me, it was a year before we actually went out on our first date. I don't remember all the details, but one thing I do remember is that it was on that date that I really saw her for the first time and realized that Michelle Griffith was someone that I desperately wanted to get to know better. That date was my first introduction to the true Michelle.

Building a relationship with Jesus is the same. Whether you come from a background where you know very little about Him or have known Him on some level your whole life, there needs to be a formal introduction, a time when we allow Jesus to show us clearly who He really is. So often, our view of Jesus is shaped by TV shows, movies, church, family, or our own imagination. It's not that these influences are bad. It's simply that a picture is painted; opinions are formed and sometimes calcified, purely on the words of others. Jesus is defined by everyone's words but His own. Before you read any further, take a deep breath, erase your preconceptions, and resolve not to blindly accept anyone's testimony about Him…including mine.

To quote my brother, Scott, "It's time to do your own research."

If you're willing to do that, you'll find that Jesus is quite capable of speaking for Himself. He makes some rather shocking and remarkable claims, and provides a test by which we can verify whether they are true. In this chapter, we are going to examine some key scriptures about Him. For these passages and all others presented in this book, I strongly encourage you to read far more than the excerpts that I present. I suggest that you read the chapters before and after so that you can understand the full context.

Lesson One

Question #1: In your opinion, who was Jesus? What is His significance?

_____
_____
_____
_____

Question #2: What is your picture of Jesus? When you close your eyes and imagine Him, how does He look?

_____
_____
_____
_____

Question #3: What comes to mind when you think of Jesus's teachings?

_____
_____
_____
_____

Question #4: What are some of His most important teachings? Are there any that confuse you or that you disagree with?

_____
_____
_____
_____

Question #5: How much of what you *know* about Jesus and His teachings is based on sermons, TV shows, movies, family, or your own imagination? How much is from your own Bible study?

_____
_____
_____
_____

Lesson Two

Video Link: www.you2church.com

Watch the First 10 Minutes of Formal Introductions

John 1:1-5

In the beginning was the Word, and the Word was with God, and the Word was God. ² He was with God in the beginning. ³ Through him all things were made; without him nothing was made that has been made. ⁴ In him was life, and that life was the light of all mankind. ⁵ The light shines in the darkness, and the darkness has not overcome it.

John 1:14

14 The Word became flesh and made his dwelling among us. We have seen his glory, the glory of the one and only Son, who came from the Father, full of grace and truth.

Question #1: If Jesus is the Word, what is the correlation between reading the word of God (the Bible) and having a relationship with Jesus?

_____
_____
_____
_____

Question #2 Do you think that it is possible to have a relationship with Jesus and not read the Bible? Why or why not?

_____
_____
_____
_____

Question #3: How often do you study the Bible? How often do you think you should study it?

_____
_____
_____
_____

Question #4: What do you think your Bible study habits say about your desire to be close to Jesus?

_____
_____
_____
_____

Question #5: What changes in your Bible study habits do you think you need to make?

_____
_____
_____
_____

Lesson Three

John 14:6

⁶Jesus answered, "I am the way and the truth and the life. No one comes to the Father except through me

John 7:16-17

¹⁶Jesus answered, "My teaching is not my own. It comes from the one who sent me. ¹⁷Anyone who chooses to do the will of God will find out whether my teaching comes from God or whether I speak on my own.

Jesus says that He is the one, but He's not the only one making that claim. He says that He is the way, but there is no limit to the myriad alternate paths laid before us. Why Jesus? Why not some other way? A good argument can be made for different religions or no religion at all. A compelling case can be made for just about anything, and the tide of contemporary morality is always shifting and changing. If anyone is trying to set his/her moral compass based on the majority, good luck. Not only is the morality of the masses constantly in flux, it is not anchored to a standard, following whatever chorus of people shout the loudest. If enough people say something loudly enough and long enough, it becomes canon. So, should I follow whoever is winning the argument? How can I know which way to go?

Is sex before marriage a sin or is that belief simply archaic and unrealistic? Is marriage the cornerstone of civilization or a cultural invention that goes against biology and has outlived its usefulness? Is homosexuality a sin, a biological imperative, or the sacred right of people to love whomever they choose? Is Chicago pizza really better than New York pizza? There are so many questions. How can we know which way to choose?

Jesus has an answer. In John 7:16-17, He says that He is the one, His way is the only way, and He can prove it. We don't have to take His word for it. What is His proof? He says that if we follow His words, we will be able to tell for ourselves whether they come from man or from God. Read them and obey them, and you will see. His way works. It works in the short run and in the long run. His way works and others don't.

The world is falling apart and all of its wisdom and philosophies are speeding up the process, not holding it together. Marriages are crumbling in divorce; lives are sinking in the quicksand of depression; families are drowning in a sea of addiction: addiction to sex, illegal drugs, legal drugs…take your pick. There is no magic in conventional wisdom. We've looked behind the curtain and the wizard of our best thinking has been exposed as a fraud. My life was in shambles, and none of my ideas, no matter how persuasive, could put it back together. My way doesn't work. Jesus does.

Jesus proposes a simple test, a scientific test. Put aside all preconceptions and tradition, read His word with an open mind and heart, and see if it doesn't touch you like nothing else. Walk with Him, the Word, and see if He doesn't change you in ways that nothing else ever has. Anyone can win a debate, can fight for a cause, or start a *holy* war. The goal is to win at life. Isn't it worth finding out if Jesus is the key to accomplishing this? Jesus invites us to follow Him, try Him on, and do our own research.

Question #1: Have you ever experienced a philosophy or point of view that sounded right but was harmful or unproductive when put into practice? What happened?

_____
_____
_____
_____

Question #2: What are some of the dangers of being influenced by the majority or the loudest voices when you determine your moral positions?

_____
_____
_____
_____

Question #3: Is there a danger in basing your moral code merely on your own personal opinions? Why? Why not?

_____
_____
_____
_____

Question #4: Would you be willing to take up Jesus's challenge and put His teachings to the test?

_____
_____
_____
_____

Question #5: What would that entail for you?

_____
_____
_____
_____

Lesson Four

Video Link: www.you2church.com

Watch from Minute 10 to Minute 17 of Formal Introductions

John 8:31-32

31 To the Jews who had believed him, Jesus said, "If you hold to my teaching, you are really my disciples. 32 Then you will know the truth, and the truth will set you free."

Question #1: Is simply believing in Jesus enough to be right with God? Why or why not?

_____
_____

Question #2: Do you ever make your feelings or opinions the driving force behind your decisions? What is the danger of that?

Question #3: What does it mean to hold to Christ's teachings? How is that different than how most people live?

Question #4: What is the relationship between being a disciple and holding to Christ's teachings?

Question #5: What are some changes you would need to make in order to hold to Jesus's teachings?

Lesson Five

Video Link: www.you2church.com

Watch From Minute 17 to the End of Formal Introductions

John 12:47-48

47 "If anyone hears my words but does not keep them, I do not judge that person. For I did not come to judge the world, but to save the world. 48 There is a judge for the one who rejects me and does not accept my words; the very words I have spoken will condemn them at the last day.

Question #1: How will we be judged on the last day? How do you feel about it?

_____
_____

Question #2: Based on John 12:47-48, is it important to study the Bible? How often?

_____
_____
_____
_____

Question #3: How important is it for the Bible to be your standard? Why is it important?

_____
_____
_____
_____

<u>Lesson Six</u>

So, if Jesus is the one, and the word is both the way we walk with Him and the standard by which we are going to be judged, what does that mean for you? As I see it, if you are reading this book, you are in one of three categories. The first option is that you are unsure about the Bible and its claims and not totally convinced that Jesus is who He and others say He is. The second option is that you are someone who believes but has never really made the time to be a student of the word and never understood its importance in having a relationship with Christ. Or lastly, you are someone who is well aware of all this and has already made the commitment to walk with Jesus daily through the word.

No matter what your circumstance, I want to give you a challenge. For the next three weeks, I challenge you to make the decision to walk with the Word daily, and see if it makes a major difference in your life. This involves reading the Bible every day, but it is more than that. Don't just read the Bible like it is a novel or a history book. My encouragement is to treat it as part of a conversation with Jesus where you make time to pray to Him and look to the scriptures for the message He is speaking to you. The question you might be thinking is, "Where should I start?" Start with one of the four gospels. I normally, suggest John, but any gospel (Matthew, Mark or Luke) will be fine. Why the gospels? Ultimately, the Bible is Jesus's story. The gospels chronicle His time on earth and give us the most direct understanding of His life and His character. In my opinion, the better someone understands the Jesus of the gospels, the easier it is to see Him in the rest of the scriptures and to understand why events, particularly Old Testament events, had to transpire the way they did. So, start with John or one of the other gospels. Put the emphasis on understanding and applying, quality over quantity. It doesn't help to read ten chapters if there is limited retention and little to no practical application. Make a three-week commitment and at the end of the three weeks, see where you are. If you are someone who has your doubts about Jesus, this is an opportunity to put Him to the test. If you are a believer but also a Bible novice, this is an opportunity to take your first step from religion to relationship. If you are a seasoned disciple, this is a chance to recommit to the basics. No matter where you are in your spiritual walk, you can benefit from your formal introduction.

Challenge #1: Are you willing to take the challenge to study the Bible daily? If so, write down your plan.

_____
_____
_____
_____

Challenge #2: Are you willing to make the Bible the standard for your life?

_____
_____
_____
_____

Chapter 3

The Love Letter

Sometimes, in the movies, two people gaze at each other from across the room and connect, instantly falling in love. Okay, that makes for a cool scene, but in my experience, that's not how it normally works. One of the differences between romantic comedies and real life is that in the real world two people rarely feel the same thing at the same time. More often than not, one party catches the love bug before the other. From that point, dog chases cat or cat chases dog until the other party catches the love virus as well or is fed up and runs the pursuer off. In my single days, I experienced all aspects of this scenario. I've been the one who chased, I've been the one who was chased away, and believe it or not, I've been the one who was pursued.

When I started studying the Bible, I realized that someone had been madly in love with me and had worked hard throughout my life to try to get my attention. God was my pursuer, and He's yours as well. He loved us first. Before we were fully formed, before we cared about Him, knew who He was, or even knew much about ourselves, God was dreaming, planning, and fighting for a relationship with each one of us. Growing up in church, I'd heard that God loved me my entire life. I guess, I accepted that as truth, but it wasn't something that affected my everyday life. It was more like a random fact than a life altering revelation. It wasn't until I really understood the cross and what it meant that I began to understand the depth of God's love for me, and that His passion for me demanded a personal response.

Imagine being back in high school and hearing rumors that some random girl or guy you had never met had feelings for you. OK, that's interesting, but for most of us, that's where it would stop. Now, suppose one day that someone gives you a letter from your admirer. This letter is painstakingly written by this person, with obvious time and care. In it is outlined how passionately this individual feels for you and the depths to which he/she would go to show the full measure of their love. Now, whether you consider this gesture romantic or more than a little stalky, I have to believe it would definitely get your full attention. The letter would not be some random fact or a footnote to your day. Whether it excites you, terrifies you, sweeps you off your feet, or makes you want to call 911, my guess is that it would invoke a powerful response. In fact, such an act of love demands a response, one way or another.

The cross is Jesus's love letter, written with His blood, with pain and tears, by His own hand. I do not believe that anyone can have any inkling of Jesus's love for him without understanding the cross, and it is impossible to truly understand the cross and its significance and not have a strong reaction. Not everyone who grasps Jesus's love letter is going to decide to follow Him, but it will invoke an emotional response and leave a life altering impression, one way or another.

Lesson One

Acts 2:36-37

³⁶ *"Therefore let all Israel be assured of this: God has made this Jesus, whom you crucified, both Lord and Messiah."*

³⁷ *When the people heard this, they were cut to the heart and said to Peter and the other apostles, "Brothers, what shall we do?"*

Acts 2:40-41

⁴⁰ *With many other words he warned them; and he pleaded with them, "Save yourselves from this corrupt generation."*

⁴¹ *Those who accepted his message were baptized, and about three thousand were added to their number that day.*

In the above passages, Peter is speaking to a large crowd on the day of Pentecost, approximately seven weeks after Jesus's death. He spoke to the crowd about Jesus with words that are recorded in Acts 2 and, according to verse 40, with many other words that are not recorded. His message was primarily about Jesus's life, His death on the cross, and His resurrection. Many of the members of the crowd were so moved, cut to the heart so deeply, that they turned themselves in, begging the apostles to let them know what they could do to set things right. Learning the answer, three thousand of the individuals who heard this sermon were baptized that day. This is truly amazing. But do you know the question that intrigues me? Why was their response to the message of the cross so different from what mine had been for so long? These people heard that Jesus, the Messiah, died for them and because of them, and it moved them to the point that the knowledge transformed their lives. I had heard the same message virtually every Sunday of my life, and it barely caused me to raise an eyebrow.

Question #1: How does the response of the people who heard the message in Acts 2 compare to your reaction to the message of the cross?

_____
_____
_____
_____

Question #2: In your opinion, what is the reason for the difference?

_____
_____
_____
_____

Lesson Two

Video Link: www.you2church.com

Watch the Love Letter Part I From the Beginning to 11 minutes 15 seconds

Question #1: In what ways would you have suffered emotionally if you endured what Jesus did?

_____
_____
_____
_____

Question #2: How does it make you feel that Jesus felt many of the same emotions that most of us would have felt in His situation?

_____
_____
_____
_____

Question #3: What do you think Jesus felt when his friend, Judas, betrayed Him? When His disciples ran off? When Peter denied knowing Him three times?

_____
_____
_____
_____

Question #4: How do you think Jesus felt when he was falsely accused and falsely beaten?

_____
_____
_____
_____

Question #5: How does knowing Jesus's emotional pain change your understanding of the cross?

_____
_____
_____
_____

Lesson Three

Video Link: www.you2church.com

Watch the Love Letter Part I from 11 minutes 15 seconds to the end.

Question #1: In your opinion, how much did Jesus suffer physically?

_____
_____

Question #2: Do you think that Jesus had the power to stop it? Why didn't He?

_____
_____
_____
_____

Question #3: How does knowing Jesus's physical suffering change your understanding of the cross?

_____
_____
_____
_____

Lesson Four

Video Link: www.you2church.com

Watch The Love Letter Part II

Question #1: How did Jesus suffer spiritually? How does this make you feel?

_____
_____
_____
_____

Question #2: Jesus became sin in order to die in your place. What are your sins that put Jesus on the cross?

_____
_____
_____
_____

Question #3: What motivated Jesus to endure all that He endured?

_____
_____
_____
_____

Question #4: What does it say about Jesus's love for you, that He was willing to do all this for you?

_____
_____
_____
_____

Question #5: What does the cross say about your true value in the eyes of God? How does that change the way you view yourself?

_____
_____
_____
_____

Lesson Five

God/Jesus can tell me that He loves me, but mere words can never express the width, length, height, and depth of His love. The cross is His love letter to me. It shows that He loved me first and loved me best, with a love that is unshakeable, unbreakable, and unimaginable. When I struggle with my self-worth, I simply remember the price that was paid for me and the fact that I am truly and deeply loved, flawed and broken as I am. I can tell someone a myriad of different aspects of what is involved in having a relationship with Jesus, but there is only one why – the cross. The love letter took hold of me and refuses to let me go.

Before reading further, it is important to understand that everything that is written next hinges on whether someone believes in Jesus and believes in the reliability of the Bible's testimony about Him. If Jesus is just a man who lived two thousand years ago, then His death on the cross, while tragic, falls in line with many other human tragedies that populate human history. If Jesus is who He says He is and He did what the Bible says He did for you and me, well, that changes everything.

Challenge #1: Take some time to pray, study, and reflect and then answer this question. Do you truly believe the Bible's account of Jesus's suffering, death and resurrection?

_____
_____
_____
_____

Challenge #2: Take some time to pray, study, and reflect, and then answer this next question. What is the acceptable response to the type of love that Jesus has for you?

_____
_____
_____
_____

Chapter 4

Crazy in Love

I love you: three simple words but man, are they powerful. Once they are spoken, you can't take them back, and when they're uttered, everything about a relationship changes. That's a lot of pressure, and it's a scary thing to be the one to share those words first. What if he/she doesn't feel the same way? What if you ruin a perfectly good friendship by jumping the gun? Worst of all, what if you get the most dreaded response in the universe, "I like you too,"? Nothing can be worse than that.

Lesson One

Before getting married, I'd been involved in other relationships, and when they ended, I'd been the one to break it off…all except one. I'll never forget how things ended with my high school sweetheart. When we graduated, we went away to separate colleges, I had it in my mind that I was in love, and that we would continue our relationship long distance, graduate and eventually get married. If I remember correctly, I'm pretty sure I had dropped those three magic words, "I love you," before we went away to school. Now, I went to college before the Internet, cell phones, and texting, so long-distance communication took the real commitment of writing letters and paying for long distance phone calls. Early in my first semester, I received a letter from my girlfriend. It was the dreaded Dear John, or in my case, Dear Frank letter. The gist: Dear Frank, let's just be friends and see other people. What? Needless, to say I was devastated, and no, if we weren't going to be together, I did not want to be friends. In fact, I don't think we ever talked or saw each other again after that (never said I wasn't petty). In truth, there's a part of me that would rather have had her say, "I hate you," than to say, "I like you," and I don't think I'm alone in that. When you are in love, the other person being in *like* is not a consolation prize. In fact, it might be the cruelest cut of all.

What does this have to do with our relationship with God? Everything.

Question #1: Have you ever been in love? What was the craziest thing you've done to show someone that you love him/her? What is the craziest thing you've seen someone else do?

_____
_____
_____
_____

Question #2: In your opinion, what are the signs that someone is truly in love?

_____
_____

Question #3: Can there be true love without sacrifice and devotion? Why or why not?

_____
_____
_____

Question #4: Have you ever loved someone who did not love you back? How did that feel? How do you think this might relate to someone's relationship with God?

_____
_____
_____

Lesson Two

Video Link: www.you2church.com

Watch Crazy in Love Part I

Question #1: What is the significance of the greatest commandment? In your opinion, why does God want us to love Him that way? Does God ask for too much?

_____
_____
_____

Question #2 Have you ever loved anyone or anything with all of your heart, mind, soul and strength? If so, who or what was it, and how was that love displayed?

_____
_____
_____

Question #3: What are some things for which you have denied yourself? What did you deny?

_____
_____
_____

Question #4: What is the most radical aspect of the devotion that Jesus demands from us? If you are honest, have you ever loved Him with that kind of devotion?

Question #5: What would you need to deny in order to love Jesus the way He calls you to love Him? What would be the hardest thing to change?

Lesson Three

Video Link: www.you2church.com

Watch Crazy in Love Part II

Question #1: What does it mean to carry your cross daily? How much devotion is Jesus calling you to have?

Question #2 Would Jesus say that He is the person or thing to which you are most devoted? What are the other things that rival or surpass your devotion to Jesus? How do you think Jesus feels about it?

Question #3: In your opinion, what is the scariest thing about following Jesus? What is the scariest thing about not following Him?

Question #4: What is the importance of someone counting the cost before following Jesus? What does that entail?

Question #5: If you're honest with yourself, have you ever loved Jesus with an unrivaled love? Have you ever counted the cost and weighed the pros and cons of totally surrendering to Him?

_____
_____
_____
_____

Lesson Four

God perfects us, through Christ's blood, in response to our full devotion; I surrender my broken life to Him and receive eternity and healing. God's grace in action is His unmerited love toward me, that He is willing to grant me unparalleled riches and immeasurable love in exchange for the toxic dust that is my life. There is only one string attached. He wants all of me.

Once I understood this, the scriptures confronted me with two questions. Had I ever made Jesus lord of my life? No, for me the answer was clearly, no. OK, that being the case, was I willing to make Him lord? Making the choice to make Jesus lord and love Him according to His love language was the best decision I have ever made. Because no matter how much I give, I can't out give Him, and I can't out love Him. Besides, He's better at running my life than I am.

Challenge #1: Take some time to study and pray before you honestly answer the question, "Have you ever made Jesus lord of your life?"

_____
_____
_____
_____

Challenge #2: If the answer to the question in challenge #1 is, No," take some time to count the cost and decide whether you are willing to make Jesus lord. If the answer to the question in challenge #1 is, "Yes," take time to reflect and evaluate whether you are still as devoted to Jesus as you were in the beginning.

_____
_____
_____
_____

Chapter 5

Being Exclusive

It is a scary thing to give your heart fully to someone and take a chance and say, "I love you," not knowing how that person will respond, but you know what's even scarier? Someone saying, "I love you, too." It is exhilarating and wonderful and extremely terrifying, a true game changer. With it comes a new set of expectations, some spoken, and some unspoken. For most couples, this involves some type of exclusive relationship. Making a decision to love Jesus also plunges us into an exclusive relationship, one with its own set of rules and expectations.

Lesson One

To help us explore those expectations, it's best that we define some terminology.

Question #1: If you had to define what it means to be a Christian, how would you define it?

_____
_____
_____
_____

Question #2: What does it mean to be Jesus's disciple? Is it the same as being a Christian, or something different?

_____
_____
_____
_____

Question #3: What does it mean to be saved? Is it possible to be saved without being a Christian? Why or why not?

_____
_____
_____
_____

Question #4: Is it possible to be saved without being a disciple? Why or why not?

_____
_____
_____
_____

Lesson Two

Video Link: www.you2church.com

Watch Being Exclusive Part I

Question #1: After watching the video, what do you believe it means to be Christ's disciple? Is your understanding the same as it was before or different? Is it possible to call yourself a Christian without being Christ's disciple? Why or why not?

_____
_____
_____
_____

Question #2: What does it mean to follow Jesus?

_____
_____
_____
_____

Question #3: What does it mean to be a fisher of men? Why is it important for a disciple to share his/her faith with others?

_____
_____
_____
_____

Question #4: Is it possible to be a disciple if one is unwilling to share his/her faith with others? Why or why not?

_____
_____
_____
_____

Lesson Three

Video Link: www.you2church.com

Watch Being Exclusive Part II

Question #1: What does it mean to love as Jesus loves? What is the most challenging aspect of that kind of love?

_____
_____
_____
_____

Question #2: Why is it important that a disciple loves his/her brothers and sisters according to this standard?

_____
_____
_____
_____

Question #3: Why is it important that God's love be the motivation for a disciple? What kinds of things can help our understanding of God's love to grow?

_____
_____
_____
_____

Question #4: Matthew 28:18-20 is called the Great Commission. What is the mission that Jesus gives every disciple in this passage?

_____
_____
_____
_____

Question #5: For you, what is the most challenging aspect of Christ's mission for his disciples?

_____
_____
_____
_____

Lesson Four

This all can be overwhelming, and what I've shared is by no means an exhaustive list of what is involved in being Christ's disciple. So, before you drop this book and run out of the room, take a deep breath. The key is to focus on *the why* and not *the what*. For the married people reading, you can understand this. If someone had given me an accurate list of everything that was involved in marriage when I was single, I'd probably still be single. If someone had given me an exhaustive list of every detail involved in parenting, I would have never had kids. The truth is, seeing my bride-to-be open up those church doors and start down the aisle (an image that still gives me chills); the details of what was expected from me were the last thing on my mind. All I could think of was that I loved her and I'd do anything for her. It was the same when each our two daughters, Jacquelyn and Kenya, were born. Holding them, my heart was filled with so much love. How could I hold my daughters and not be all in? Once I fell in love, real love, everything else was just details. At that point, fully invested. Focus on the love, and the rest will come easy.

This is the same for our walk with God. If you haven't done it yet, take the time to get to know Jesus and fall in love with Him. If you focus on *the what* and lose sight of *the why*, you will end up with empty, burdensome religion, and that never saved anyone. Decide on *the why*, and *the what* comes easy. Yes, disciples are called to imitate Christ's life, and yes, we are called to make disciples, but that is not really the point. The point comes down to three simple questions. Does Jesus love you? Do you trust Him? Do you love Him enough to give your life to Him? If you want my advice, do not focus on the details of what God expects until you decide what your answer is to those three questions. The why has to come first. If you get to know the real Jesus by gazing into the heart of the one who died for you, you will fall in love. How can you help but be all in? How can you help but to surrender all to Him and share this love with others? This is the essence of the two greatest commandments; everything else hangs on these. Focus on the love and the rest comes easy; everything else is just details. With that being said, I am not trying to minimize the fact that Jesus cares very much about us being obedient to these details. But truthfully, once someone is motivated by Christ's love, obedience to His commands is a joy not a burden.

Challenge #1: Now, that you've studied what it means to be a disciple, take some time to pray and reflect before you answer the next questions. Would you say that you've been a disciple of Jesus up until this point in your life? If the answer is, "No," are you willing to become Jesus's disciple?

_____
_____
_____
_____

Challenge #2: If you decide that you want to be a disciple, what changes do you need to make in order to be a disciple of Jesus? Take some time to pray, reflect, and devise an action plan.

_____
_____
_____
_____

Additional Scriptures Concerning Discipleship

Luke 9:23-26, Matthew 22:37-40, Luke 10:25-28,

Luke 14:25-33, Luke 9:57- 62, Luke 13:22-25,

Mark 1:16-20, John 8:31-32, Acts 11:25-26,

Matthew 28:18-20, John 13:34-35

Chapter 6

The Engagement

Being engaged is the time in a relationship where everything becomes more serious - DEFCON 1 Level serious. The idea of sharing vows and making a permanent commitment to someone is equal parts exciting and daunting. For one thing, wedding planning is a dizzying, mind-boggling adventure. No matter how much time a couple has to plan for it, it is never enough, there are so many details. There are even more specifics to discuss when two people are working through the particulars of merging their lives. Topics that may not have been breached or even thought about now have to be carefully vetted. My place or yours, or do we get a new place together? What furniture are we keeping? How do we manage our finances? Everything, I mean everything, is about to change. To the unmarried men contemplating matrimony, let me give some life advice. It is far more valuable to make your bride happy than to have your way. Don't be too attached to your favorite couch, that comfy chair, or even that favorite sweater (my wife took me shopping and gave me a makeover when we got married; I never saw it coming.). It is different for every couple, but the one constant is simply this: for two people to come together, some stuff has to go, and some new things are going to be added.

Lesson One

So, how does this relate to having a relationship with God? Becoming a disciple is the greatest decision anyone can make, and it is the most important. Like marriage, when someone decides to follow Jesus, he has to make a decision to subtract some behavior from his life and add some as well. Before making this commitment, one has to decide whether the benefits of following Jesus are worth enduring the challenges.

Question #1: How would you define sin? Is there such a thing as big sins and little sins?

_____
_____
_____
_____

Question #2: What are some examples of big sins? What are some examples of little sins?

_____
_____
_____
_____

Question #3: If you are honest, are there commands in the Bible that you find unfair or unrealistic?

Question #4: What does it mean to repent?

Question #5: In your opinion is there a relationship between repentance and being saved? If so, what is it?

Lesson Two

Video Link: www.you2church.com

Watch The Engagement Part I

Question #1: According to the scriptures, what is the effect of sin on our relationship with God? Scripturally, is there such a thing as big sins and little sins? Why? Why not?

Question #2: Read through Galatians 5:19-21, Matthew 5:27-30, and II Timothy 3:1-7, taking time to look up the definition of any words where the meaning is not immediately clear. What are the sins that stand out to you? Are there any that surprise you?

Question #3: What are some sins committed by others that have hurt you? How were you hurt? What hurt you most deeply?

Question #4: What sins have you committed that have hurt others? How were they affected? From your point of view, what is the worst thing that you've ever done?

_____
_____
_____
_____

Question #5: In chapter six, I shared how sin led to brokenness in my life. How has sin led to brokenness in your life?

_____
_____
_____
_____

Question #6: How do you think your sin has affected Jesus?

_____
_____
_____
_____

Lesson Three

Video Link: www.you2church.com

Watch The Engagement Part II

Read through: Matthew 5:27-30, Luke 13:1-5, II Corinthians 7:8-11, and Acts 26:20

Lesson Four

The scriptures from the previous lesson and many others clearly articulate the importance of repentance. It is both the key to healing and a necessary step in accepting Christ's grace. In an article for ThoughtCo.com, Jack Zavada offers the following definition, stating, "Repentance in Christianity means a sincere turning away, in both the mind and heart, from self to God. It involves a change of mind that leads to action-- the turning away from a sinful course to God."

The Eerdmans Bible Dictionary defines repentance in its fullest sense as "a complete change of orientation involving a judgment upon the past and a deliberate redirection for the future."

Ultimately, although most people normally discuss repentance strictly in terms of turning from sin, it really encompasses every aspect of the decision to leave one's old life and fully dedicate himself to being Christ's disciple. In many ways, repentance is a synonym for lordship or surrender but it has inherent in its definition the practical application of those concepts. If Jesus is truly lord, then radical changes need to take place in order to conform to His example. These changes involve every aspect of our lives, both thought and action. Lordship demands that some habits must be cast off and others must be added, and repentance is the decision to follow through on the promise of Jesus being lord by surrendering the details of who we are to Him.

Luke 13:2-5 makes it clear that there is no salvation without repentance, no being born again until we decide to kill and bury our old lives. I've heard it said that salvation is achieved by simply accepting Jesus as your personal savior, but Jesus did not request permission to be my savior. He demands to be my lord. When Jesus became my lord, He became my savior because everyone under the authority of His kingdom is redeemed by Him. For so many years, I wanted the benefits of God's eternal kingdom without fully submitting to His authority. In his masterful book about repentance, *Repentance: A Cosmic Shift of Mind and Heart*, Edward Anton reminds the reader that both John the Baptist and Jesus open the proclamation of the gospel with the command, "Repent for the kingdom of heaven has come near." Of this, Anton writes, "For only a cosmic shift of worldview affords us a view of the kingdom of heaven." Without repentance, a relationship with God is impossible.

Question #1: What does it mean to repent? What is its significance? Is your understanding of repentance different after studying this chapter? How?

_____
_____
_____
_____

Question #2: What are some areas where Jesus is calling you to repent?

_____
_____
_____
_____

Lesson Five

Acts 3:19

19 Repent, then, and turn to God, so that your sins may be wiped out, that times of refreshing may come from the Lord,

Repentance is our part, but the heavy lifting belongs to Jesus. As Acts 3:19 clearly states, the wiping away of our sin and the times of refreshing come from the Lord. Try as we might, even making every effort, we cannot change ourselves, the roots go too deep, and the call of our inner demons is too strong. We cannot break the chains of sin, heal the wounds from our past, or learn a new way of being simply on willpower and determination. It is the redeeming power of Jesus's blood that washes away our sins and the supernatural power of the Holy Spirit that makes transformation possible. But this is the interesting part: God respects our free will. He will not deliver us until we desire it with all of our heart and soul. Repentance is an acceptance of God's grace and an invitation for him to act on our behalf.

I imagine that God was working throughout my life, trying to get my attention, longing for the day when I would truly turn to Him. He longed to redeem my soul and heal my wounds and to free me from my anger and fear, but He needed me to do something first: surrender. Once I truly understood, surrendering to Him was not a cost. It was a rescue. But before I could get to that point, I needed to take a long hard look at the scriptures and see what they said about me. The Bible is a mirror, and it will show us ourselves, our true selves, if we let it. There is no transgression too egregious, no addiction too strong, no wound too severe, and no curse too dark for God to overcome. He is able and willing to save. The question for me and for all of us is are we ready to repent, or at the very least, are we ready to take a good look in the mirror?

Challenge #1: Now, that you've studied what it means to repent, take some time to pray, reflect and devise a plan for repentance.

_____
_____
_____
_____

Challenge #2: If at all possible, choose a mentor or a close friend who can be an accountability partner for your plan of repentance.

_____
_____
_____
_____

Additional Scriptures Concerning Sin

Galatians 5:19-21, Mark 7:20-23, Romans 1:24-32

I Corinthians 6:5-11, I Corinthians 6:15-20, James 4:17

James 5:16, Luke 18:9-14, Ephesians 5:3-13

Matthew 5:27-30, Hebrews 10:26-27, Colossians 3:5-11

Ephesians 4:29-32, II Timothy 3:1-7, Revelation 21:8

Genesis 4:6-7, Romans 7:14-25, Matthew 18:21-35

Additional Scriptures Concerning Repentance

Luke 13:1-5, Luke 3:7-14, Acts 26:20

Isaiah 57:15, Colossians 3:12-14, Acts 3:19

II Corinthians 7:8-11, Psalm 51:16-17, Romans 8:5-13,

Acts 2:36-38, Psalm 51

Chapter 7
The Wedding

The wedding day: what a special day. Michelle and I had a fabulous wedding. OK, honestly, I don't remember most of it. It was a blur, and I was an emotional mess. The one thing that I do remember and I will never forget is when the doors of the church building opened and Michelle started walking down the aisle, with sunbeams and angels ushering her in. Wow, I almost had a Denzel Washington man tear go down my cheek. It was an amazing moment. In this world, there is no shortage of opinions about marriage and weddings, and among them are an increasing number of voices that argue that marriage is not essential, but the Bible leaves little room for ambiguity.

Lesson One

God created marriage, and He likes weddings. In Ephesians 5:21-33, Matthew 19:1-12, and elsewhere, the scriptures share God's views on the subject. For Him, marriage is essential; a permanent, binding covenant between a man and a woman. Over the years, I've spoken with many couples where one party (generally the man) disagrees and would minimize the importance of matrimony. Many a man has told me some version of the following, "What's the big deal about getting married? I love her; she loves me. We live together and function as husband and wife in every way. What would be different if she had a ring? Why does God care if we have some stupid ceremony? Aren't we married in the eyes of God?" I reply by answering the last question first. No. You are not married in the eyes of God. After that, I show the couple scriptures and teach them about God's views on the subject, and I talk to the man privately about the real reasons he is avoiding marriage because there is always a deeper reason. One of the, legitimate, underlying questions people have on the subject is how can a ritual mean so much to God? By definition, isn't a ritual merely symbolic?

The wedding is a ritual, but not all ceremonies are created equal. My wedding band is purely symbolic; other than tradition and sentimental value, it has no meaning. Placing it on my finger was part of our ceremony, but taking it on or off does not affect whether I am married or single. The wedding itself, however, is something different. The Bible does not give a specific procedure for marriage. The actual make-up of the ceremony is different for every culture, and the Bible passes no judgment on this. But the Bible does place enormous value on a couple following their cultural customs, obeying the laws of the land, and declaring their union before God and man. Yes, marriage is a ritual, but it is not merely symbolic. The scriptures say that the two become one flesh and cautions, "Therefore what God has joined together, let no one separate"(Matthew 19:5-6). The two start the ceremony single and leave married. There is no magic in the venue, the officiant, or the words spoken. The ritual has power because God makes it so. Through an act of grace, He bonds two souls and seals them in a covenant relationship during that moment and time. It is a gift and a promise that He reserves for those who stand before Him in holy matrimony. I guess He could do things differently. He could offer this gift to anyone who whispers, "I love you," under the sheets, lives together for a period of time, or has a joint checking account, but He has chosen not to. God is sovereign. Two becoming one is His gift to give, and He has chosen to empower the ritual of marriage and reserve His blessings and this gift for those who partake in it. We can argue with Him, but in the end, the voice of the Alpha and Omega is the only one that matters. Now, I'm sure you're wondering what this detour about marriage has to do with building an intimate relationship with God. It has more to do with it than most people think. Jesus instituted His own version of a wedding between Him and His disciples, and many of the same principles apply.

Question #1: In your opinion, why does God put such an emphasis on a couple being married before having sex and/or living together?

_____
_____
_____
_____

Question #2: What does the importance of a couple's wedding teach us about God?

_____
_____
_____
_____

Question #3: What does it teach us about the importance of obedience?

_____
_____
_____
_____

Lesson Two

Video Link: www.you2church.com

Watch The Wedding Part I

Question #1: Is there anyone who deserves to be saved? Why or why not?

_____
_____
_____
_____

Question #2: Is there anything that you can do to earn your way to heaven? Why or why not?

_____
_____

Question #3: At the end of the day, what is the determining factor concerning whether an individual is lost or saved?

_____

Lesson Three
Video Link: www.you2church.com
Watch The Wedding Part II

Question #1: Does it surprise you that repentance is connected with receiving the blood of Christ? Why or why not?

Question #2: What is baptism? What is the role of baptism in connecting with Christ's blood?

Question #3: Is it possible to be baptized scripturally without first repenting? Why or why not?

Question #4: Is it possible to be baptized Biblically, if someone has not decided to be Jesus's disciple? Why or why not?

Question #5: When is someone ready to be baptized? What decisions should someone make before being baptized?

_____
_____
_____
_____

Question #6: If someone is baptized who has not first repented, is that truly a baptism?

_____
_____
_____
_____

Lesson Four

Matthew 28:18-20

18 Then Jesus came to them and said, "All authority in heaven and on earth has been given to me. 19 Therefore go and make disciples of all nations, baptizing them in the name of the Father and of the Son and of the Holy Spirit, 20 and teaching them to obey everything I have commanded you. And surely, I am with you always, to the very end of the age."

Matthew 28:18-20 contains some of Jesus's final instructions and this passage makes it clear that baptism is very much part of His plan. When one has faith in Jesus and repents, deciding to turn from self and embrace discipleship, Jesus calls him to be baptized. An individual is not a candidate for baptism until he has decided to make Jesus Lord. But the question before me was how could I claim that Jesus was my Lord if I resisted the command to be baptized in His name? What would be my reason? Tradition? My pride? My fear? I was baptized in November on a weekday. I had spent most of the night reading scriptures and praying about my decision. I went to my classes, fidgety, already having decided what I was going to do. It was either a Tuesday or Thursday. There were no services scheduled at the church building where I had begun to worship. I did not have a car, and the building was over a half hour walk from campus. This was before the time of cell phones and the Internet, so advanced planning was extremely important, and I really did not have much of a plan other than my urgency to obey what I had read. I had not thought it all through as far as the mechanics. I just started walking to the building the minute classes were over, determined to find someone in that building to baptize me. I showed up and spoke to the receptionist who was able to locate the campus minister. He asked me a few questions, wanting to know if I understood the seriousness of my commitment, and then asked if I wanted to wait and take more time to think about it. "No," I answered, "I'm ready. I want to be baptized, now." Now that I knew what Jesus wanted, I did not want another day to pass by outside of His promise. It was around 3:00PM. A few of my friends from the Bible study showed up, and minutes later, I was baptized. It was my wedding day, a special day. OK, honestly, I don't remember most of it. It was a blur and I was an emotional mess. The one thing that I do remember and will never forget is that I felt the presence of Jesus and His love and I was determined to love him back with everything in me and never let go…no turning back, no turning back.

Challenge #1: After prayer and Bible study, answer the following questions honestly. Have you ever been baptized scripturally? If the answer is no, what do you think Jesus wants from you? What, if anything, is holding you back?

_____
_____
_____
_____

Challenge #2: If, after study and prayer, you believe that God is calling you to be baptized, answer one question. Are you ready to repent of your sins and be Christ's disciple? If the answer is yes, find a disciple in your area who can baptize you. If you need help finding a group of disciples in your area, please feel free to contact us: thejesuslovestory@gmail.com and we may be able to assist in connecting you with a mentor.

_____
_____
_____

Challenge #3: If you do get baptized, send us a picture or video of the baptism. We love wedding pictures.

_____
_____
_____
_____

Additional Scriptures Concerning Baptism

Acts 2:36-39, John 3:3-6, Matthew 3:13-15,

Matthew 28:18-20, I Peter 3:20-21, Mark 16:16,

Colossians 2:11-12, Galatians 3:26-27, Romans 6:1-7,

Acts 8:26-40, Acts 9:17-19, Acts 22:15-16,

Acts 10:44-48, Acts16:13-15, Acts 16:31-34,

Acts 18:24-28, Acts 19:1-6, II Kings 5:1-19

Chapter 8

Meet the Family

Most people do not wait until after the wedding to meet their significant other's family. Generally, at some time during the courtship, normally after the relationship has become serious, the couple will meet each other's people. Michelle's mom loved me (hey, who wouldn't?), but my mom absolutely adored Michelle, and my wife became her adopted daughter. In fact, I honestly believe she liked Michelle a whole lot more than she liked me. I guess that could have made me feel insecure, but then we had children, and my mom doted on her granddaughters and totally forgot about both of us. That, my friends, is the circle of life. I share this because when we got married, we not only married one another, we became grafted into an extended family, in all its dysfunctional glory. Becoming a disciple is much like this.

Lesson One

When we are baptized into Christ, we are baptized into His family, and it is impossible to have a relationship with Christ without having one with His brothers and sisters. The idea that walking with God is purely vertical, just between the individual and God and nobody else, is foreign to the Bible. When we are born again, we are born into a brand new family. God is our father, Jesus is our brother, and every disciple is our brother or sister, and how we treat our brothers and sisters has a direct bearing on our relationship with God.

I John 4:20-21

²⁰ Whoever claims to love God yet hates a brother or sister is a liar. For whoever does not love their brother and sister, whom they have seen, cannot love God, whom they have not seen. ²¹ And he has given us this command: Anyone who loves God must also love their brother and sister.

Question #1: Is it possible to be close to God and have little or no relationship with other Christians? Why or why not?

_____
_____
_____
_____

Question #2: What do our relationships with our brothers and sisters in the church say about our relationship with God?

_____
_____
_____
_____

Lesson Two

Video Link: www.you2church.com

Watch Meet the Family Part I

Question #1: What is the church? Is it possible to be close to God and not be connected to the church? Why or why not?

_____
_____
_____
_____

Question #2: What are some reasons that it is important for you to be connected to the church?

_____
_____
_____
_____

Question #3: How does the church benefit you? How does it benefit other disciples?

_____
_____
_____
_____

Question #4: Why is it important for you to not just attend church but also be actively involved?

_____
_____
_____

Lesson Three

Video Link: www.you2church.com

Watch Meet the Family Part II

Question #1: Does it matter where you attend church? Why or why not?

_____
_____
_____
_____

Question #2: What are some characteristics of a Biblical church? How important is it to attend a church based on the model in Acts 2:42-47?

Question #3: Do you regularly attend church? If so, how does the congregation compare to the model in Acts 2:42-47?

Question #4: Do you believe that your discipleship can prosper in your current church environment, or do you need to search for one that is more grounded in the principles of discipleship?

Question #5: According to scriptures, what priority should you give church attendance and involvement? How does your current level of involvement compare to the Bible's standard?

Lesson Four

So, as a brand new, baby Christian, it was easy for me to see how I needed the body. Everything was new to me. Every Bible study, campus devotional, and worship service taught me something new, and the time I spent being mentored by more mature Christians was invaluable. I understood how I needed them. How did they need me?

We all have a role, each and every one of us. We have unique gifts, talents, and perspectives. In addition, our journey, with all of its successes, failures, joy, and pain, is something strictly our own. Whether I felt it or not, I was special, and designed with specific purpose, and had an ordained role to play in building up Christ's body that was exclusively mine, and that was as true as a one day old Christian as it is thirty-four years into my story. Even way back then, there were needs in the congregation that I was created to fill, people I was there to encourage, individuals who my journey would inspire, and problems that my unique perspective was adept at identifying. As time went on, I gradually noticed issues and needs, and sometimes wondered why not everyone saw what I was seeing. It finally dawned on me that God had allowed me to see these things because He wanted me to do something to help. I could either sit in the back of the church and be critical, or be part of the solution, more importantly be part of my Lord's plan. I was a member of Christ's body. When Jesus desired to give a hug, he would use me, if I let him. When He wanted to address a need, reprimand sin, mentor the lost, or encourage the hurting, He would speak through me. I was there for a reason. This is equally true for each and every disciple of Christ. For disciples, church is not just something that we attend. We are the church. We are a family of imperfect, surrendered souls, bound by grace, our love for the Lord, and our love for one another. As each part does its work, the body grows and prospers, and more light is spread into this dark world.

Challenge #1: If you are not currently a devoted member of a Biblically grounded congregation, take some time to search for a local congregation that is devoted to the Acts 2:42-47 model. If you need assistance, our Love Story staff may be able to help. Feel free to email us at thejesuslovestory@gmail.com

_____
_____
_____

Challenge #2: Once you are connected to a local congregation, spend some time in prayer, and if you have not already found one, identify a spiritual mentor who can aid you in your walk.

_____
_____
_____

Challenge #4: Once you get plugged in, send us a picture or video of your church family. We love seeing our brothers and sisters around the world.

_____
_____
_____

Additional Scriptures Concerning the Church

Acts 2:42-47, John 13:34-35, Ephesians 1:22-23,

Ephesians 2:19-22, I Corinthians 12:12-26, Romans 12:3-13,

Hebrews 10:23-25, Matthew 18:18-20, Matthew 6:33,

Colossians 1:17-18, I Corinthians 1:10-13, II Timothy 4:1-5,

Chapter 9

Next Steps

So, I met Michelle, got to know her, fell madly in love, met her family, and somehow, conned her into marrying me. So, was that the end of our story? Hardly. Twenty-nine years later and we're still going strong. It has been a wild ride. No, the wedding wasn't the end. It was the end of the beginning. My journey with Jesus has been the same. My baptism was the end of one life and the start of another, something better. It ushered in a new chapter of my adventure, and I've been learning to live a spirit filled life ever since. So, now that we've reached this point in our story, what are the next steps? Thankfully, for this too, the Lord left instructions.

Matthew 28:18-20

¹⁸ Then Jesus came to them and said, "All authority in heaven and on earth has been given to me. ¹⁹ Therefore go and make disciples of all nations, baptizing them in the name of the Father and of the Son and of the Holy Spirit, ²⁰ and teaching them to obey everything I have commanded you. And surely, I am with you always, to the very end of the age."

As stated earlier, I've been blessed with being married to Michelle, an amazing woman of God, for almost three decades, and we have two beautiful daughters. I know this is all from God. Left on my own, with my sinful nature and emotional baggage, none of this would have been possible. I know something else. Without the men who took me under their wing during my first two years as a Christian, my life would have been very different. They were there when I was most vulnerable, when my faith was new and untested. These brothers were obeying Matthew 28:18-20, particularly verse 20, not simply teaching me about discipleship and baptizing me but staying involved in my life and leading me to spiritual maturity. For a young disciple, being mentored is an important next step, and for mature disciples, it is important to be a mentor and give back what has been given to you. Spiritual maturity, learning to become disciples who make disciples, is the goal. If you are interested in building on the lessons learned from this book, I have five scripture inspired next steps to recommend.

1. **Stay in Prayer and Bible Study:** The most significant decision that you can make to aid in your spiritual growth is to walk with Jesus daily. It should be your first priority to have daily conversations with the Lord, talking to Him and listening to Him. Remember, prayer and obedience is how we speak to God, and the word is the primary way that He speaks to us. Make time, daily, to speak and listen. Tools can help. Hopefully, both the book, *Love Story*, and this workbook, have served as useful tools. In addition, there are two other books that I can recommend: *Passing It On* (a series of studies that can serve as either devotional times or a study guide for a mentor and student), and *Closer Than a Brother* (a book that will assist in learning more about discipling and one another relationships). Both books can be found at the website www.jesuslovestory.com

2. **Find a Church:** If you have not done so, find and connect with a church devoted to disciple making and sound Biblical teaching. Study Acts 2:42-47 and other scriptures concerning the body/Christ's church and seek a church committed to the Biblical model. If you currently attend a church but feel it is not devoted to these principles, please, do not hesitate to look for another. Finding a life giving body of believers is one of the most important investments you can make for your spiritual journey.

3. **Find a Mentor:** Depending on where you are in your spiritual journey, it is important to find a mentor or become one. Matthew 28:18-20 shows that spiritual mentorship is part of God's plan. Look for someone who is a true disciple of Jesus, not simply knowledgeable and religious. In our broken world, disciples have a tendency to stand out. Seek someone who has a solid grasp on the word, whose righteousness and walk are inspiring, and who has a desire to invest in you. This can be one of the most rewarding relationships of your life. Equally important is that after you have reached a level of spiritual maturity, you find someone to mentor. Discipleship is designed to be a gift that keeps on giving.

4. **Share What You Know:** You don't have to be a Bible expert to share what you do know and what God has done for you. We are commanded to go, and there is no time like the present to put that command into practice. Share your knowledge, share the tools that have blessed you, and share your story. God can use you where you are today to be a blessing to someone else.

5. **Tell Us Your Story:** If *Love Story* has been a blessing to your life, we want to hear about and share your story. Email us at **thejesuslovestory@gmail.com** with your written or video testimonial, and we will post as many as possible on our website www.jesuslovestory.com, and on social media.

If you are ready to be Jesus' disciple, prepare for the greatest adventure of your life. As Jesus's co-workers, we get to be curse breakers. Sin is the gift that keeps on giving, but so is love. But here is the key: to make a difference, you must risk something; to change the world, you must risk everything. Go and together let us share the *Love Story* to a broken world, helping it be a little less broken one story at a time.

Bibliography

Coleman, Robert E. <u>The Master Plan of Evangelism</u> 2nded. Grand Rapids: Fleming H. Revell a division of Baker Book House Company, 1963.

Anton, Edward J. <u>Repentance: A Cosmic Shift of Mind & Heart</u> Waltham: Discipling Publications International, 2005

Jacoby, Dr. Douglas (2013, July 31). *A (more accurate) Medical Account of the Crucifixion* Retrieved From https://www.douglasjacoby.com/a-more-accurate-medical-account-of-the-crucifixion/

Davis, Dr. C. Truman. *A Physicians View of the Crucifixion of Jesus Christ* Retrieved From http://www1.cbn.com/medical-view-of-the-crucifixion-of-jesus-christ

McClister, David (2000, January). *The Scourging of Jesus* http://www.truthmagazine.com/archives/volume44/v440106010.htm

Driscoll, Mark (2014, April 4). *How Much Did Jesus Suffer? A Medical Account of Death by Crucifixion* Retrieved From https://www.charismanews.com/opinion/43525-how-much-did-jesus-suffer-a-medical-account-of-death-by-crucifixion

All About God.com (2002-2017) *What is Sin* Retrieved From https://www.allaboutgod.com/what-is-sin.htm

Ybarra, Thomas, R. (2014, April 14). *Repentance On Sunday for What One Has Done on Saturday* Retrieved From https://quoteinvestigator.com/2014/04/14/repent-day/

Zavada, Jack (2017 March 6). *Repentance: What Is Repentance in Christianity?* Retrieved From https://www.thoughtco.com/what-is-repentance-700694/

Trotter, Andrew, H., Jr. *Grace* Retrieved From https://www.biblestudytools.com/dictionary/grace/

Fairchild, Mary (2017 June 28). *Definition of God's Grace: What Does God's Grace Mean to Christians?* Retrieved From https://www.thoughtco.com/meaning-of-gods-grace-for-christians-700723

Jacoby, Dr. Douglas (2016 January 28). *Baptism Basics (Part I)* Retrieved From http://www.disciplestoday.org/bible-study/digging-deeper/item-7705-douglas-jacoby-baptism-part-1#.WlPFzyOZO7Y

Lotha, Gloria (2009, May 5). *Legion* Retrieved From https://www.britannica.com/topic/legion

<u>The Hebrew-Greek Key Word Study Bible</u>. Chattanooga: AMG Publishers, 1996

www.ingramcontent.com/pod-product-compliance
Lightning Source LLC
LaVergne TN
LVHW061217060426
835507LV00016B/1979